THE FISH IS IN THE NET

PAPERBAGE

PROLOGUE

We publish this book with the good intention of sharing how to share knowledge. We believe that sharing knowledge is undoubtedly one of the most current issues, one of the objectives of improvement that all organizations have on their agenda, but at the same time, it is something that still seems alien and strange to most of them. Maybe because we feel that it is too abstract of an idea that never comes intro fruition, that it is good intentions that we do not know how to put into practice every day.

And that is exactly what we want, to put our feet on the ground by linking theories with practice. We have recovered, because of their validity, old ideas of classical theories. We have discovered, because of their novelty, new theories to explain the new age of information. We have combined them, on our own, and we have created a new recipe with all those ingredients. They have served as the basis to develop and propose a set of diagnostic, design and communicative action tools. They are tools to facilitate communication between people. We have completed a puzzle in which the pieces fit us. We have put them in practice, some of them partially and at reduced scale, and finally, we have wanted to spread them to find more people willing to work with us, either by putting them into practice or by helping to develop them.

In the first part of the book, we focus on defining knowledge, as we understand it. In addition to that, we explain how to make an initial diagnosis of the flow of knowledge - if there is one - and the types of learning established in an organization.

In the second, we propose how to design the network on which the knowledge will flow.

In the third and final part, we present our communicative action tools where we say *approach is everything*. We discovered that there is a suitable approach for each communicative need.

Finally, we note that we have written the book trying to use a colloquial, intimate tone for a more pleasant reading. We hope we have achieved that.

Any person or organization interested in participating, collaborating or developing our proposals can contact us by sending an email to this address: paperbage@gmail.com

PAPERBAGE

Index

PAPERBAGE

What is knowledge?

To correctly answer this question, we turned to the experts. Specifically, in our original work in Spanish, we had to consult the official dictionary of the Royal Spanish Academy (RAE).

It tells us that knowledge is, in its true meaning, the action and effect of knowing; although the dictionary adds additional meanings, such as understanding, intelligence and to have a notion of or know of something.

That is something at least. Something like the capacity that human beings have to understand the reality, nature and the world around us.

Simplifying, so to speak, knowledge is what we know. Well, we can say with more accuracy and more detail, but as a definition to jump-start it to us.

And since we are starting to look back, let us start from the beginning. Because everything was simpler before. Remember how the world was before the Internet. That time, a distant time ago, where knowledge resided in books, or if we refer to people, scholars, authentic walking libraries, also known as 'bookworms,' a breed that is already an endangered species.

Education was eminently mnemonic. Logically, in that environment, anyone that was able to store as much knowledge in his or her brain was the person who was better prepared.

Then came the Internet and its universal knowledge. It put itself within everyone's reach.

What did this mean? That suddenly we were all wise? That all of a sudden, we enjoyed superior knowledge and at the highest level? Of course not! It only meant that it was available if, said metaphorically put, you would just stretch out your hand and you knew what you wanted to grab, grasp and pick up.

Just because it was within reach, it did not mean that everyone could use it, it just meant that whoever was able to discern, to differentiate, to seek, to classify or to find it, could use it.

Some experts say that at the present moment, knowledge grows exponentially. Apparently, it is difficult to know exactly, but some say that in ten years, it doubles in number. Some argue that it is even faster, that this doubling occurs once every five years. Consequently, this would mean that any graduate or a graduate fresh out of University has expired knowledge even before starting to work. It would mean the knowledge taught in college was already out of date. The gap is monumental, sidereal, huge, and almost insurmountable.

Now you have other ways to get knowledge that is up to date, and not behind the times. You can take an online course with MIT, an Oxford course, a course online based in Sydney or even in Logroño, Spain. You can receive the latest advances and discoveries related to your work just sitting at your computer. You can follow cutting-edge research almost live. No need to wait several years until a German publisher sells its publishing rights to a publishing house from your country; something so juicy that is happening in Hannover or Dusseldorf. You just have to hit a key. There are no excuses. You can do it. We can do it. Anyone can.

Now, the most important skill is knowing what we want and how to find it in the tidal wave of net.

Information and knowledge await us in the cloud, they are waiting for someone to give them meaning, since information and knowledge, on their own, without the subject, are nothing but bits, zeroes and ones in apparent disorder, floating in virtual space. This, with the permission of Artificial Intelligence, written in capital letters, which, any of these days, will have gotten the best of us.

But we continue without making a sense of it all. We are blocked! What is wrong with us? If everything is right there! Now, experts say - there are still a few, of course! - knowledge comes from the web, it just needs somebody to find it, to jump like a dolphin.

But we have a problem. Or more. And thinking about that, what would life be like without problems? We have so much where to search and find that the very abundance has become our greatest obstacle. If we do not have any food, we starve, but if we eat too much...oh boy! If we eat too much we suffer from indigestion. Having too much information is as problematic as having almost none. Right. But scarcity was worse, the difficulty of access and control of the information by the few. That is why we think that we complain about this situation out of habit. This is the one.

Therefore, let's get to work. Cast your fears away. Live the moment. Plunge into the ocean of knowledge and data, dive and emerge completely soaked in knowledge. And share it. Because life is also about that. Above it all. Sharing.

The world has changed radically. In our times, in the age after the Internet, it is said and remarked that the true wealth of organizations is their shared knowledge.

And it is true, yes. One must share. And learn by sharing. Because keeping knowledge and information for yourself, as top secret or something indecipherably arcane ready to use at the right time to take us to new heights does not work. We wander through deserted plains in a world full of spontaneous synergies and collaborations.

Since everything changes so fast that we cannot stop and think that the process of learning has concluded, no one can say that he or she knows, that he or she has finished learning, we are immersed in an uninterrupted and unfinished succession - also endless - of continuous training. Thinking about it is almost vertiginous. But it is like this in all fields of human activity, in all fields of human knowledge. As it was once said: We will rest when we die.

We propose to make a diagnosis of the flow of knowledge existing in our organization - as bad as it can be, there must be some intelligent life- to then be able to design better paths and pathways where knowledge can flow smoothly. Because according to George Siemens, the key is in knowledge flow, the recognition of patterns in a sea of complexity, the creation of meaning through learning networks.

Horizontal one is more comfortable than vertical

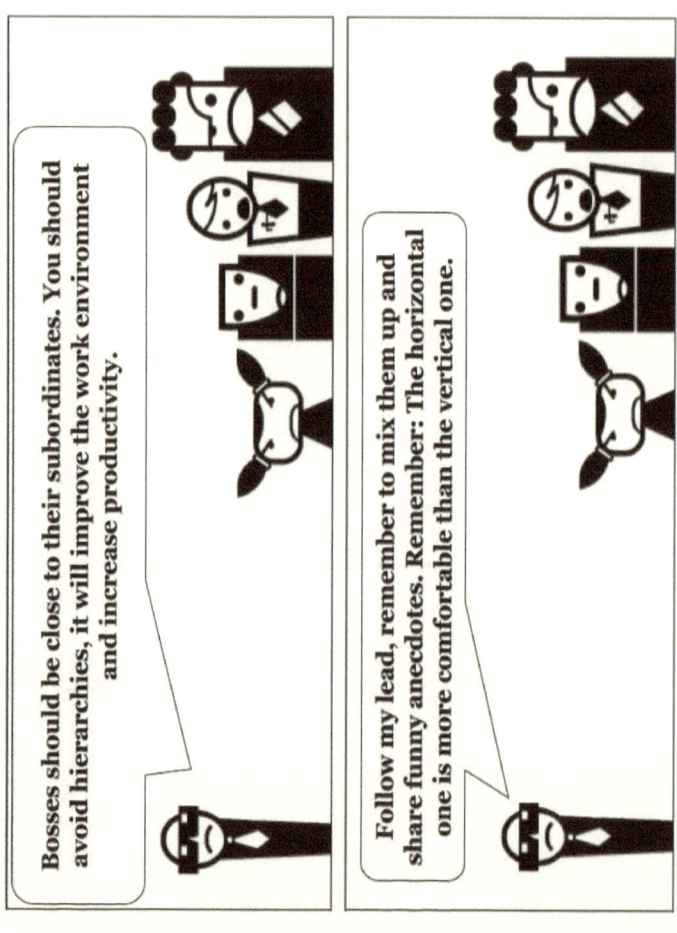

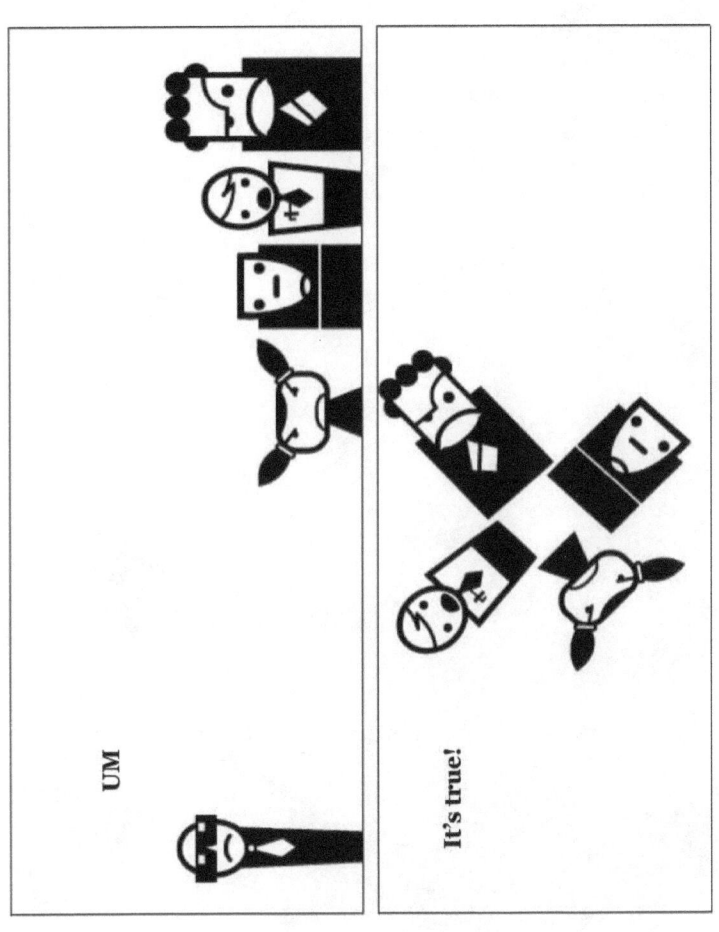

It is like this in many cases. Try going uphill with a bike super-fast or, climbing up some stairs to the fourth floor. We will not continue giving examples. As the someone once remarked: There is no need for more words. This is a direct consequence of Earth's gravity. And Newton warned us about it. He explained it. But everyone else knew about it. Many times, we know things without knowing why they are like that. It was known.

Just as we know water flows downhill. Rain falls down. And everything that goes up, goes down. Then, why would it be different with knowledge and wisdom? Is knowledge some kind of gas that is lighter than air? Is knowledge like Helium?

Of course not, the natural direction of knowledge is just that, the one determined by gravitational forces. Or there might be other forces at play. Yes. There must be others, but with a visible reality to those with eyes on their faces. The one above says things to the one below. The one above knows something, he is up there for a reason and he is not down there with the one below, who is down there for some reason as well.

This kind of primary thinking and crushing logic is the what still works in most organizations.

Many time - way too many - we have seen that, as soon as they have ascended, they climb a step or go up in hierarchy, a wisdom halo surrounds the climber, like a sanctity ring. He goes from knowing nothing to knowing in record time.

This has been this way for a while, and it still remains so to some extent, and we are getting by. Because we can see the shape of the organizational chart in our organizations, we can see that they look like the Giza pyramids. This is not only because often they resemble the pyramidal triangular shape, but also because of their colossal size and the secret chambers and corridors yet to be discovered.

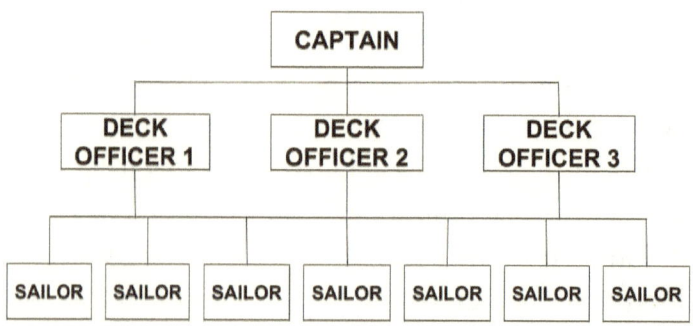

The question we ask ourselves, since we are doing this, regarding knowledge in organizations is: how does this - knowledge- flow inside these stony structures resembling one of the seven wonders of the ancient world?

In a cascade! Information tends to adopt the shape of the structure it rests upon. This is almost a physical fact if we think about great skyscrapers that host multinational corporations.

This *cascade* effect is not negligible, and it should not be underestimated. It is efficient when there is an endless source of knowledge at its apex, on top.

Is that our case? Do we have the Nile Springs above our heads, and we have not even suspected it until now?

Or, following the aquatic metaphor, has the drought dried up the sources, completely exhausted, squeezed dry and nothing flows down anymore?

No need to go far to see such a phenomenon. Organizations that were once the leading ones because of their added value no longer know, they are simply unable, nor do they even pretend to want to transform themselves by their willingness to maintain the market captive by other means -many times spurious and monopolistic- but they don't last too long as there is not much more of a future other than the inevitable collapse.

Therefore, if an organization is to survive, stay afloat and adapt to changing times, it must become more horizontal and less vertical so that it is the true manna of our times. Perhaps it always has been this way, but now it goes faster - it is shared knowledge, the flow of shared knowledge which is our proposal.

We propose to make a diagnosis of the flow of knowledge within the organization. We propose to graphically represent the organigram and the conductive threads that link the departments, their interactions, their methods and effective management of existing vectors.

We propose to travel through the designed network using several communicative action tools that profoundly transform the organizational culture so that knowledge sharing is the norm, the usual. In other words: how we are, how we want to be and how we make the transformation.

Types of learning

Just as Watzlawick insightfully told us in his first axiom of the Theory of Human Communication *it is impossible not to communicate.* We could simultaneously assert that it is impossible not to learn.

Which is fortunate, because it makes things much easier for us to achieve fluid knowledge.

It is impossible not to learn and we learn without realising it since birth. Learning abilities are innate. It is in our DNA

We learn to speak easily ever since we are little. And then it gets more difficult. Several centuries ago, Fernandez de Moratín -the father- was amazed by French children learning to speak perfectly without difficulty.

> To speak in a foreign tongue,
> A Fidalgo in Portugal,
> He gets old and speaks coarsely,
> And here a boy speaks it

An acquaintance of ours, dedicated to teaching, commented to everyone who would listen, after several decades in his office he had concluded that children learn despite teachers.

Our friend said categorically that far from belittling the job of an educator, he made it made more relevant. He had to strive not to place unnecessary obstacles on that natural process. It had to provide a suitable habitat, environment and optimal conditions for development. A question which was not a trivial one, he added, with the current ministerial education programmes, with minimum taxes paid by so-called experts in the field. It was 'one size fits all.' Look, in spite of everything, they learn.

This is important to know. We are made for this. We have an overdeveloped brain. Some of us have bigger heads-some more than others, why deny it-even if sometimes head circumference is not aligned with intelligence, but by greater capacity to attack, as the poet Antonio Machado was in charge of reminding the Spanish before their Civil war.

We have varied learning theories that draw colourful landscapes according to the taste of the expert on duty which tries to explain to us how the brain functions throughout this procedure. Truth be told, we believe we are still far from explaining what the exact and detailed brain mechanisms involved, but they can serve as a roadmap.

It is crucial to ask what the types of learning are in organizations. Because, initially, it is essential to be aware of the way that information and knowledge travel, that is, from where and where and which way it goes according to the network and, on the other hand, how they are received and retained, how they are internalised and how they are learned.

Does the subordinate command and subordinate him or herself? Does he or she teach the command and learn the commandment? ¿Does the one in command know a lot and there is no one to teach him or her? Does the one below want to learn? Does the veteran meet the novice, for what? Does the veteran act and the rookie take notes? Does the rookie act and the veteran corrects? Does the veteran act and the rookie proposes? Do they operate at once or divide the work and collaborate amicably? Are they together or separate? In short, is vicarious learning by imitation? Or just observational? It is cooperative or competitive? Collaborative or competitive? Or is non-existent? No, to clarify- did we not agree that it was impossible not to learn? There are many questions in search of answers.

We propose to identify existing processes and modes of learning in organizations in order to further improve them by specific approaches.

We know that organizations have long been concerned about this issue. Craftsmen's guilds of the Medieval villages took special care in regulated learning. They distinguished between masters, journeymen and apprentices, depending on the veteran and the skill acquired in the craft.

At present, the main trends for organizational improvement programs have been training and total quality programs implemented in many organizations.

There is a whole industry specialising in aid and improvement. Some of it, quite a lot actually, we learned on our own. Every so often, we all have had to retrain, rethink, reinvent, restructure. We have to admit, with satisfactory results.

In rare cases we have met our best expectations. Most times, too many times, we have yielded a sovereign waste of time, that unknown substance that expands or contracts according to our mood.

Why would you do that? No doubt because of the erroneous approach of these activities: their uniform design -the same for everything, the vertical tilt-from top to bottom, or its uncompromising corset - according to the scarce budge, for its non-existent practicality -too theoretical and far from everyday reality-, by its associated marketing -giving priority to advertising titles, certifications, medals and distinctions- and for other reasons that we cannot think of right now, but you know well.

We will propose another way, we believe quite different, to address the issue. Get closer. If you have that kind of hunger for knowledge, you only need a fishing net.

PAPERBAGE

The fish is in the net

As we think we have clearly expressed our preference for the horizontal position and our most resounding rejection of the Egyptian pyramids, the next step, logically, must be to explain the horizontality i.e., how we conceive communicative relations denuded of any distortive hierarchy.

And our answer is the network. A network designed to facilitate the flow of knowledge among all members of the organization.

Of course, the network we propose can coexist seamlessly with other flowcharts designed and used for other functions.

Live and let live. We will not destroy or overthrow the senior officials or strip the chiefs of their functions, but we will design an ecosystem, a parallel network, with its own rules and regulations, as a separate installation of ducts and hot water pipes or air conditioning inside a building that serves only the laws of fluid dynamics or dispersion of gases.

Although we will not deny that obviously this new facility can influence and change the previous structures to adapt them for better performance.

How does one configure the internal network of the organization? Our answer is to talk about networks, we will start with Euler.

Euler was a Swiss mathematician of the eighteenth century who made many contributions to science. Among them is the formula called Euler's identity which encompasses all transcendental numbers into a sum of zero result.

$$e^{i\pi} + 1 = 0$$

Known as 'Euler's Identity,' it connects 5 commonly used numbers in math. A success worth of his genius.

A formula with profound meaning and most certainly, still with an unknown reach.

Certainly, less known but more useful in our case, Euler also developed graph theory, which provides us with the right tools to explain what we mean by an organization that is well designed, connected, and better equipped to share knowledge.

Euler faced a problem that will surely be of great interest to the parcel deliverymen so abundant in our Amazonian times.

He stated and solved the famous -yes, famous and known, even if you did not know it, (not everything is about you), the problem of the city of Konigsberg (now Kaliningrad) and its seven bridges.

Well, we may exaggerate the notoriety of this man, who besides being well known by other mathematicians for the 'Venn diagram,' if we could not look him up on Wikipedia, we would not know if *Venn* was his last name or the name of a collaborator.

After looking it up, we see that they were not compatriots- since Venn, with two *'ns' was* an Englishman and they were not even contemporaries - Venn came later-.

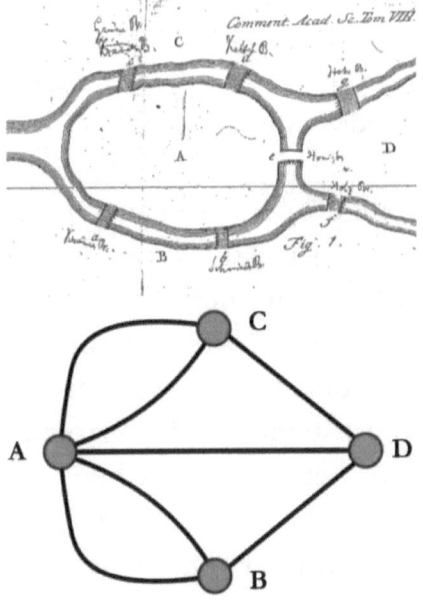

The original city plan of Konigsberg used by Euler in his demonstration.

Below, the corresponding graph, in which node A and D represented the two isles, node C the Northern bank and B the Southern one, the edges on the other hand, would become the seven bridges that linked the different spaces of the city.

Euler, in his search for the shortest route, showed that it was not possible to cross all bridges passing through all of them just at once. Incidentally, he founded graph theory. Surely, he could not imagine while walking along those bridges that all those ideas would become so successful as to what would eventually become the study of networks. You never know nor can be almost sure of anything. Forgiveness, except in mathematics, where everything is accurate and provable.

Let us see how mathematics behaves this time. Let us see if they serve to catch on or enhance organisation. Let's make an explanation as brief as possible with illustrations for you to understand better, not to bore you with so much wording.

Graph theory uses edges and vertices. The vertices are the network points or nodes. The edges are lines connecting the nodes -the wide points, for absent minded.

Nodes, according to edge orientation may be a source of- they give something to another node- or well- or receive something from another node.

(Open parenthesis. Those of us of a certain age without going into too much detail- when we hear the word *node* we cannot avoid listening to background music with trumpets and kettledrums, while we remember a gentleman of short stature with a moustache and a sash, peering over the railing of a swamp. Close parenthesis)

Next. You can subtract the well index from the source to determine the contribution index of each node. Thus, we will have positive or negative nodes, depending on your contribution in the network.

Nodes with several edges of different origins are multigraphs, which, by the way, for the objectives we have, would be a sign of quality directly proportional to the number. Even duplicate edges between two nodes can be indicators of quality, demonstrating different routes of connection between two nodes.

In this mathematical theory, the path between two nodes is called a path, even when passing through other nodes. Therefore, the following types of graphs are considered according to the number of direct connections or indirect ways, with intermediate nodes:

A graph is connected if there is a direct connection or at least one *path* (Through other nodes) between any nodes.

LINKING GRAPH   **NON-LINKING GRAPH**

In the linking graph, there is a linking path between all the nodes, from node 1 to node 5 (passing through intermediate nodes 2 and 5). On the contrary, in the non-linking graph, nodes 4 and 5 are completely disconnected from nodes 1, 2 and 3.

A graph is complete when there are direct connections between all nodes. A graph is strongly connected when there at least two different *paths* between any nodes.

Another relevant concept is the network

STRONGLY CONNECTED GRAPH

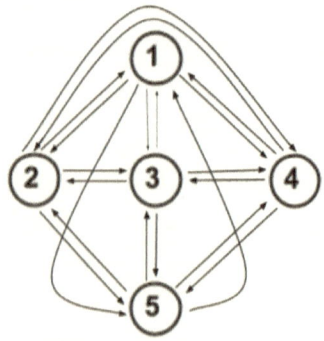

In the strongly connected graph all the nodes are directly connected among themselves, without intermediary nodes, at least in two ways and directions.

diameter, which is the distance between two nodes, that is, the fewer edges or lines in the *path* between two nodes. You can get the average diameter of a network with the average distances between nodes.

This indicator reflects the complexity of a network. Low average indicates the closeness and the high value of shared knowledge. A high average may indicate a large extension or complexity of the network.

The graph can be interpreted positively or negatively depending on the circumstances. The social network analysis by graphs can check position, centrality and importance of each node (social actor or knowledge that is defined as such a node) within the network. It teaches us the power structure, links, orientation, intensity and the shape and direction of transmission of knowledge, information or sometimes the centres of power, and other things.

Edges have a mono or bi-orientation and their morphology is very important. It must be analysed on those grounds; that is *how it* is between nodes. Nodes must be well defined, that is, what each node represents. All this can be represented graphically, or by arrays and lists.

We propose that the network should consist of a complete and strongly connected graph. That is, each and every one of the nodes or edges of the graph must relate to all others, if possible, by two edges at least.

Nodes can represent people, places -charts, forums-, books, On the other hand, edges may represent different ways of interacting and communicating, speaking, writing, listening, leave a message, a file, a video...

That is, in summary, the net where the fish is collected, where the cod is cut.

THE ANALYSIS OF
THE NETWORK
USING GRAPHS
REPRESENTS
THE INTENSITY,
THE MORPHOLOGY,
AND THE
ORIENTATION OF
THE TRANSMISSION
OF KNOWLEDGE

PAPERBAGE

The development and growth of the NETWORK will be our main objective. To do this, we will detail the steps you can take to build your own personal network, and if you are not satisfied with this, we will explain what strategies are appropriate so that your environment is also able to organize itself in the form of a collective network.

After describing these networks, we will introduce communicative action tools that you can have and use for the successful development of such networks. Some tools or approaches that when following an analogy with another network - the road network - would become its traffic code, traffic signs, transport vehicles, train and bus schedules. Thus, being a valuable example for its explanatory value.

PLENK

We have all met a colleague of a profession totally detached from their professional field. People working on their own as always done, with no flexibility and adaptability to zero improvements or changes that occur in their own area. They are discouraged people, sometimes too rigid, often insecure or fearful about the future. Other times they are just lazy and do not want to make the effort. In the end, what for? Is it going to involve some personal change? Is it being valued tangibly -in cash or in some kind, in your company? Is it worth it the effort?

We are entering uncharted territory which we will later refer to as the 'attributive approach.' Let us leave it for later. If your curiosity is gnawing at you, you can move forward looking at the index, which is there for a reason.

As we mentioned, there are people who do not worry about their training, which as time goes by, it is more relevant than ever, and should be ongoing.

No matter how well designed the network of the organization is, if some points (the wide nodes corresponding to the idle one), provide nothing new and are a well or sink of the negative index, this is an indication we aren't doing well.

A reminder. To clear any questions or deepen the concepts we are using, you can consult the bibliography at the end of the book. I'd have a look if I were you.

We need an ecosystem in which people are motivated by the work of providing and sharing fresh knowledge that enriches the plural network, eager for new blood as a Transylvanian vampire.

Let us describe the training motivated by staff. For this, the following concepts come in handy: PLE (Personal Learning Environment), PLN (Personal Learning Network) and PLENK (Personal Learning Environments Networks and Knowledge).

Let us look at one part at a time. This type of person is a person who is responsible for him or herself in various aspects that until now had been the responsibility of the organization.

Until very recently, all organizations were designed vertically from top to bottom, their training plans conveniently aligned with objectives proposed, once again, from the top.

What happens now is that that knowledge directed from above and received by the underdog is knowledge that largely does not need to be shared, because of another coffee for everyone- once again -, with some variants of milk and tea, everything has to be said. We do not say it is wrong, no. But just as we had with cups of coffee and coffee substitutes and what we urgently need are other options. More variety with the menu, please.

Now it comes to sharing the plural and diverse knowledge, while we are already saying that the network is plural and that is why we need people who are able to self-organise their own training. People who are accountable to catch up in their field.

People who are updated, not outdated as a hair dryer -programmed obsolescence not only applies to appliances, no. People willing to share what they catch, receive and learn in their personal network. People willing to share their own personal network.

Let us check the previous acronyms. The first is the personal learning environment (PLE), the second personal learning network (PLN) and third (PLENK) personal learning environments, networks and knowledge, - a hybrid of the two.

While initially used for children's educational environments, today we can expand its field of action to any type of learner.

This kind of responsible person-learner- can have their virtual network -specialized web sites, professional forums, scientific magazines, national and international meeting points, online classes...- and its physical network - talks, live courses, meetings, conferences...- and they can share it.

Of course, this should be rewarded in some way. This is possible only in an environment that facilitates, promotes, values and rewards.

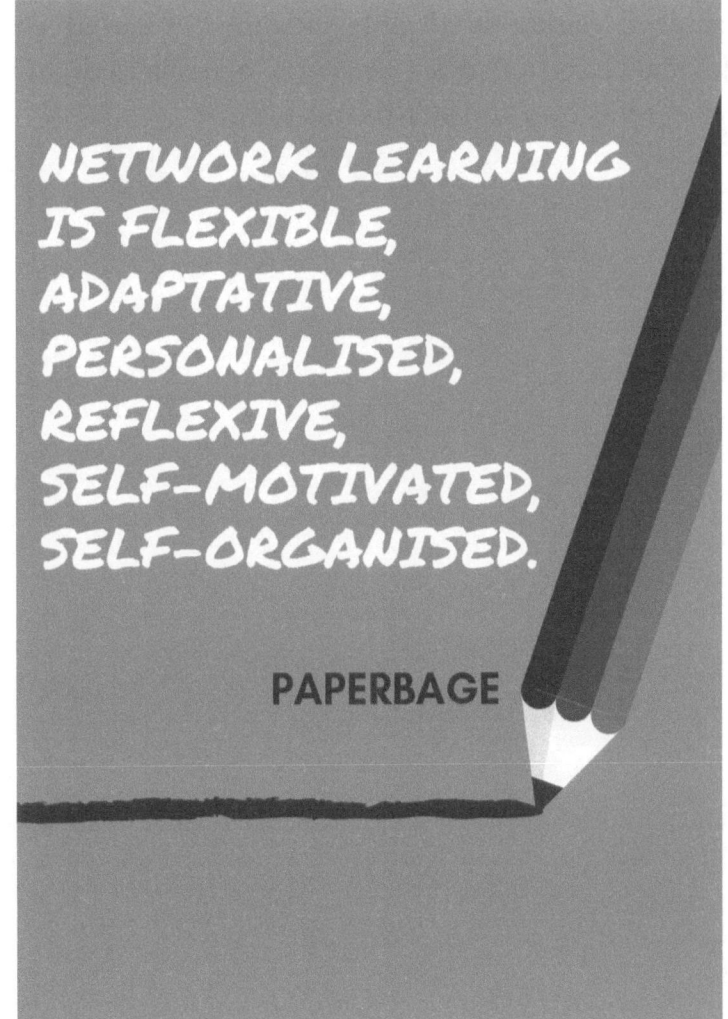

To specify the woven netting, to some extent, it's an undressing. To explain procedures, spaces and innovative content found to whom is interested is no small feat. This type of learning because of its self-organized nature is flexible, adaptive, focused on personal characteristics - *customised,* personalised- and invites reflection and self-motivation.

Dedicated spaces

Another pill of nostalgia- Who remembers those radio programmes in which you called in and you could dedicate a song to your Mum, your girlfriend or even request a liturgical prayer like the sursum corda (of course we are speaking about here in Spain).

Those times in which there was a bolero song for your Spanish grandmother, then a rock song like ACDC, followed by some folk and Demis Roussos! It was a special space dedicated to all your musical favourites. They gathered us around together with the radio on, and sometimes it coincided over lunch or after dinner, because in some stations it was what was after a little something in Spain we call the 'Angelus;' for others it was in the afternoon, just before the Holy Rosary (again, another Spain analogy). We were surrounded by religious events. We used to record the ones we liked on cassette. Those badly recorded cassettes in which the announcer's voice sneaked on at the beginning of your favourite song, but you didn't care because it was your own compilation -your potpourri- and you listened to it until you knew it by heart.

This is due to the fact to we have made an association of words between the next point, the spaces, and the dedicated songs.

Let us leave the nostalgia for another moment once we have properly introduced the subject at hand.

We propose to establish *spaces* of convergence, confluence, union and meeting.

Of course, we just checked a web page of synonyms that has helped us to extend the list of nouns. They come in handy, since they all add different nuances, within the similar meaning, and give us more clues in relation to what we are proposing. We call them dedicated spaces. Dedicated to what or to whom?

Siemens teaches us that spaces are in themselves agents of change since changes in spaces change procedures.

In addition, the spaces can become nodes, very wide points that help us configure the network we are designing.

We know that it is not the same to place the tables in one direction, in a U shape or in a circle. It is simply not the same. This distribution of furniture which would be the most obvious, is just a small sample of what we are talking about. We can go much further, and we are not limited to geography or furniture ergonomics per se.

The variety of possible dedicated spaces is unlimited. Fact is, what we've been excited about is actually very limited. Limited to what can happen to all of us and that suits the goal of weaving the network. Let's say they can be virtual-a mailing list, a WhatsApp group, a Facebook page, Google Drive, a specialized forum. Perhaps even physical, with square meters in space-time: a reading room, a wall with a blackboard, an assembly hall, or even a simple room. They can be objects-a book of any kind, a table, etc.

These can be dedicated spaces structured conveniently for innovation, for training or self-training. They can be centrally located or distributed, or self-created spontaneously and freely. The most important thing is that they can be -to the extent that they can be the network and also will be the network. They will be both. There will be fish: Tuna, Sardines. Mackerel, Anchovies, and Bream - there must be everything, even Salmon. A bit of everything.

PAPERBAGE

Are all meetings the same?

Maybe all the meetings you have participated in have been the same. We could even put an ellipsis after it and let each one add what eschatologically applies. You may have just changed places, the meeting has had some interruptions, some of the attendees have got up and left, but it seems to you that you are still in the same meeting since the first time you met.

And the reason is that you almost always do the same thing in every meeting. Of course, they are not identical, but they are very similar. Perhaps let us compare it to the similarity of one drop of water to another.

What will the boss want? Normally someone from the top ranks is the one who calls the shots and decides on the agenda. Much like news writers who meticulously grab the attention of the reader with a flashy headline. The boss reels you in from the beginning all the way to the finish line of the meeting in which he decides exactly where that is.

Sometimes they capriciously show a democratic façade by giving different options to their subordinates having their opinion openly interpreted so whoever wants to understand can understand, and those who cannot are left to the wolves.

The paradox of the subject occurs when they seem to sincerely assume that ideas or alternatives contribute and they do not take into account that you are qualified and well-trained, thinking you don't know, nor are you interested in knowing, and thus incapable.

Although of course, in the case of proposals, they will decide, because they are the ones who know how to chaff from the wheat.

The topology of the meetings speaks for us. Its geography, or where we are located are allotted only for a select few and there is no other way around it. The varied nature of the fauna invites you to choose. There are small groups of old dinosaurs, happy little groups of young rookies, old lonely sea lions, the suck-ups, The chief's bodyguard and his gregarious hyenas, and elusive herbivores grazing aloofly in meetings. Tell me who you sit with and I will tell you who you are. Each one identifies with their kind and this is how inbreeding is reinforced, encouraged, and perpetuated.

Each one acts his part, his role internalised during long hours of meetings, a role that is played over again and again.

Some always carry the singer's voice, always opinionated, many times ranting, dictating the next line, and demanding to be heard.

What's wrong? Do they believe that all meetings are assemblies? Do they need to be heard?

Those of us who, by age or place of birth, come from a pre-democratic space-time, lamentably remember those assemblies and noisy meetings in which everything has been passionately debated and voted on. Some perhaps because of their past feel compelled to express their opinions about everything and assert their position of power. They are a type of spokesperson often aligned with power and sometimes in opposition to power. However, they are always dogmatic enough to mark pre-established paths which lead the group to a black and white dilemma, to a simplification of the issues in question.

Others do not say anything, they shut up and concede, following the self-proclaimed spokespersons in their harangue, either because they have no opinion of their own, or because on occasion they agree. On other occasions they dare not contradict them, either because they prefer non-confrontation, or to stay in their comfort zone. In the end, for what?

We propose that formal meetings be structured and have a fixed, clear, and known objective which is planned beforehand. In addition, according to the objective a different way of doing things can be applied.

For this reason, we propose different approaches. These would be approaches that facilitate communicative action; thus, being able to share knowledge of all the participants that contribute to their corresponding roles.

The Approach

The approach is key to meetings. Define meeting: we would say it is any agglomeration of people always consisting of two or more people. Whichever be the purpose- Expressed with breadth and without restrictions.

On the other hand, when we talk about approach, we are referring to the act of being concentrated, focused, and that is to say with the necessary energy and attention that is required to fulfil an objective, the extent to which we are involved.

Or we can refer to the point of view, to the location where we place ourselves to look and address a topic, the perspective we adopt. Both meanings are undoubtedly complementary to the question at hand.

We propose to use appropriate approaches to the proposed objectives. The different approaches we propose are tools of communicative action that aid us in improving our communication because not all meetings are the same.

On the one hand, we have the work and responsibility of the organizer of the meeting, the collusion, the gathering, the gossip, the 'tell me what you know' guys.

Since ancient times we know before this frenzy of organizational improvements began that preparation in advance helps to achieve objectives.

There are three old friends known by everyone. First, having a previously known agenda made in enough advance by all participants; second, an adequate moderation conducive to the proposed objective that avoids useless detours; and third, a final act that summarises the conclusions.

All of this which seemed ideal to us and majority of the times we did not comply.

It is totally inadequate from our point of view. Let's accept that we are a nullity in these meetings. We are a zero to the left.

THE KEY TO
THE MEETINGS
IS TO USE THE
APPROPRIATE
APPROACH FOR
THE PROPOSED
OBJECTIVES

PAPERBAGE

THE FISH IS IN THE NET

On the one hand there is the preparation of the meeting's agenda. There are many meetings (and I will try and be nice when saying this), the meeting was ill prepared, and the organiser was not so inspired. There are others in which there is no such thing, directionless, wild birds who were called to the meeting and do not know if they come as dinner guests or as a featured item on the menu.

There ought to be some sense and be guided by common sense- if we lack it, it is something that has no remedy - and that all participants receive it in a timely manner so that they can prepare their possible interventions.

Because that is what it's about, is it not? Also, those summoned must attend to their previous duties. And of course, they are competent.

It is true, we tend to be lazy in some respects. When we don't see practicality, or think that something is a waste of time, an inner voice tells us: What are we doing wasting time?

The act is not written, or if it is, then it is not read. Or if it is read, nobody hears it. Or if it is heard, the audience nit-picks. There are unfulfilled agreements, delayed deadlines in relation to what is foreseen in writing, and nothing happens.

We propose to positively value the compliance of the minutes recorded and their resolutions rather than ignoring or punishing breaches. The philosophy of positive rewarding is our friend and is the most recommended criterion.

Clearly there are different types of meetings and some would say at least half a dozen according to the most versed and read lists on the Internet.

All right. And what do we do that we do not apply? Because if we repeat them again, all the meetings seem to be the same.

We propose different roles rather than the types of meetings where we must explain our approaches. We focus on criteria and communicative principles adaptable and compatible with other approaches. Because more than talking about informative meetings, meetings for innovation, meetings for debate, etc., we will also talk about approaches with predetermined roles.

Any meeting can be organized according to a specific approach that facilitates the attainment of the predetermined objective.

It's a drawer! We do not know why it had not occurred to us before!

But if we already did that – the naïve guy at the back would say - he still confuses the approach with the objective of the meeting. Which is like confusing the fate of a trip with the way we travel.

But let's not run too fast that we begin to get out of breath. We can take this step by step. What do we understand by 'role'?

Apart from being a neologism, more specifically a Gallicism which is a new word of French origin -the worth of pedantry- can be understood in several ways.

Years have passed since we were assaulted by sensational news about teenage role-playing games, tragic news in which young people immersed themselves in role playing and committed Grande acts of violence, alienated by the plot in which they participated in- a mixture of episodes in which they did not clearly distinguish what was real from what was fictitious.

Those young people, it could be said, were almost abducted by their own characters and this created a huge social upheaval, or perhaps it was the journalists? Overtimes these stories have lost their momentum and media presence

We have known other more bearable or less dramatic roles. The actors play roles or roles in the works. It has also been common to use role-playing in language learning, especially in methods based on communication.

Someone will tell us that he has sometimes played the role of son-in-law at Christmas dinner, the socio-cultural entertainer for nieces and nephews, the devil's advocate, or party pooper, all dependent on how lively his family and social life are.

The first thing that comes to mind when speaking about this topic is the classic Chaplin quote stating that "life is a play that does not allow testing." We all represent different roles in life, some almost simultaneously. We are children, parents, partners, friends, enemies, colleagues, etc. We are everything Chaplin's quote is emphasising. Maybe we rehearse even if only in front of a mirror, talking to one other aloud, preparing a talk we will have later.

Surely Chaplin hinted at a broader sense 'to rehearse,' but as far as our subject is concerned, we have no doubt that if we prepare, rehearse, and anticipate, at minimum we can improve our roles.

All of these meanings that come with the term 'role,' help us to understand what we are going to talk about, ergo the preamble as a starting point. We are going to break down what we understand by *focus* and *role*, both concepts united indefectibly and inseparably in our proposal.

The Dialogical Approach

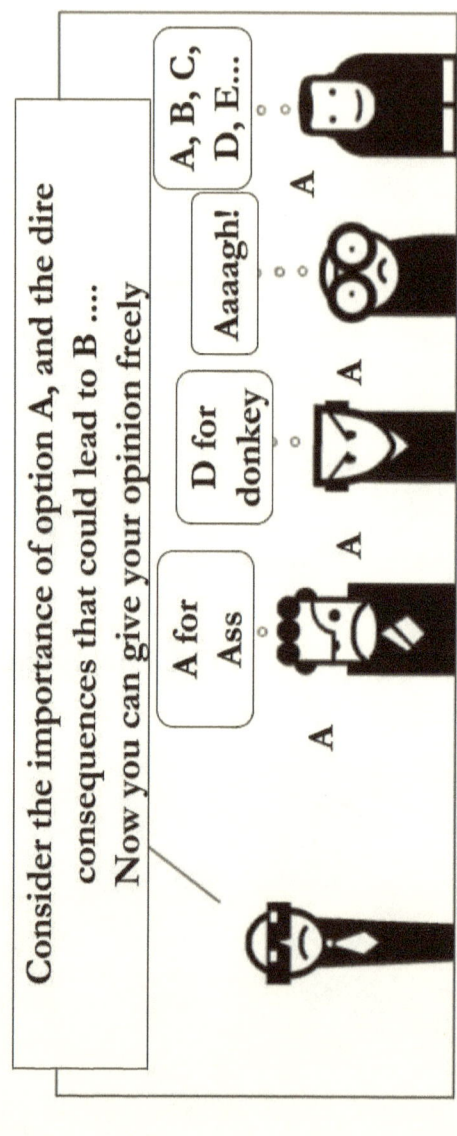

Recall those times in which Western liberal democracy was valued for its diversity of opinions. Let us remember how communism of the Soviet bloc was being reviled, giving unanimity to the Bulgarians as an example of lack of freedom.

How could they all agree? It was impossible. They were not free. This was demonstrated by the lack of logical dissension in political decisions.

However, without reaching such extremes, in the last few decades we are leaning towards a kind of suspicious unanimity, dictated by the politically correct. It is as if we always want to agree or act as if we're in agreement.

It has gotten to such a point that in some tricky issues dissenting opinions are unacceptable. You arrive at a modern-day witch-hunt in which you disqualify anyone who goes off the marked path. A narrow path in which you must parade in a politically correct single file.

Consensus is something that we do not care much about. Sometimes we can worry about negative things, on the behalf of another. However, it is not that we are necessarily against it. This is not the central idea around which our proposal revolves around.

While it is true that even Habermas defends consensus as necessary for communication, we think that we must limit it to specific moments or phases.

CONSENTS IS OVERRATED, IT IS VITAL TO AGREE THAT THERE ARE DISCREPANCIES.

PAPERBAGE

If it is not circumscribed to certain phases, consciously and deliberately separated, it clashes with the concept of plurality. And it is from this plurality that we must build consensus.

In the same way that it is usually practical to reach consensual agreements, we should not confuse the imposition from minute one with the agreements taken after exploring all possibilities.

In any case consensus in communication has its place, by no means is it worthless, in deliberative and decisive moments.

We want to talk about freedom of expression without fear of what they will think and what they will say. We divulge free speech as the basis of our proposal and as an indispensable and versatile tool as a means of obtaining knowledge.

Since classical antiquity, great names have used dialogue as an indispensable instrument to acquire knowledge.

Socrates is a model of what we are talking about- tireless speaking even at the risk of bothering staff, all the way until his tragic end. A model of what the ancient Greeks called 'parrhesia.'

Parrhesia was to speak freely and audaciously. It was to feel obliged to say the whole truth, without omitting any bits and pieces left in the nooks and crannies of the mind. It was a bold sincerity in which we could express our truth without fear or hesitation and keeping to the objective of the common good without fear of putting yourself at risk.

Now we propose that the truth is better because it is worse. It is more credible, more plausible, closer to everything human, and downright imperfect by nature.

We are inclined to think that truth is more honest, especially if it is accompanied by a portion of healthy self-criticism. Above all messages within the organization itself since complacency usually hurts us.

Using a cinematographic reference, we will quote Mr. Lobo from Pulp Fiction, when Travolta's character was astonished by his efficiency in cleaning a totally blood drenched car. He is reprimanded with the following sentence: "Well, let's not start sucking each other's dicks just yet". For those who barely speak English it could be something like: let's not celebrate too early, (or something like that).

And yet we inflict a lot of pain on to ourselves. We are always thinking about what others are going to think, about the consequences of our actions and our brutal honesty. or this, we say what is expected to be said.

In an organization in which parrhesia is to be practiced by everyone it seems okay that for even those who work in subordinate positions or who are located lower in the food chain, can speak their truth and nobody be surprised.

But without looking so far we have other good precedents in the last half of the 20th century. As Habermas proposes, all human knowledge or all truth, is a communicative action between subjects that is based on sharing some assumptions through language, agreeing on some valid pretences.

However, in certain environments communication is distorted because of different aspects, when only reason can be the principle of true communication.

ALL HUMAN KNOWLEDGE
OR ALL TRUTH, IS A
COMMUNICATIVE ACTION
BETWEEN SUBJECTS THAT
IS BASED ON SHARING
SOME ASSUMPTIONS
THROUGH LANGUAGE,
AGREEING ON SOME
VALID PRETENCES.

HABERMAS

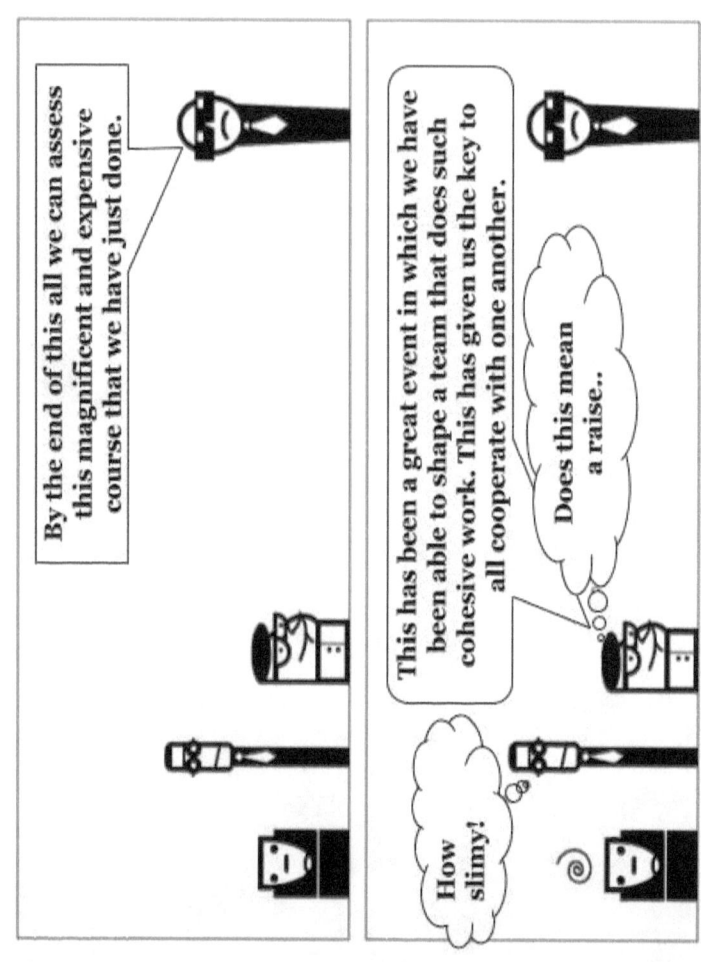

In most organizations, perhaps all of them including progressive organizations, there are situations in which discourse is one of domination and repression. It is not frank and open dialogue.

And that is because the propitiatory conditions do not exist and the tools that can prevent it are not used.

On the other hand, in the same sense, we contribute the vision of the Brazilian Paulo Freire, who alongside his pedagogy of the oppressed was made known to the last years of Francoism with his message. He influenced several generations of teachers. Freire disagreed with the builders of German holocaust camps- in which the front signs famously read, "work will set you free."

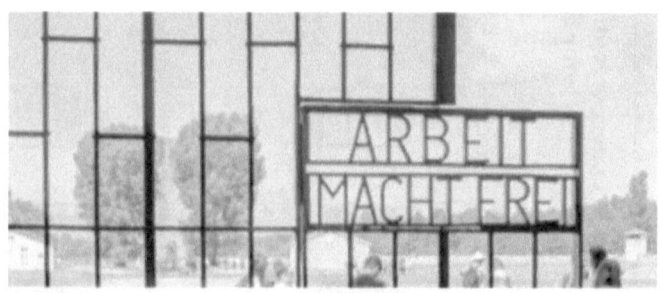

The entrance gate of the Sachsenhausen concentration camp, which reads in German, "Arbeit macht frei."

Let's say that he didn't agreed with neither form or concept. Freire thought that education gave resources to the poor and oppressed so they could prosper in life and break the yoke under which they suffered. In other words, education freed him.

Among many other ideas he advocated he was very successful during those years. But the key idea that Freire gave us is that we all learn through dialogue, which not only the student learns, but also the teacher. This can still result in some shock. There are people who don't understand it in its proper measure and importance. There are a lot of them, and this is the truth.

In his theory of dialogical action, he postulated that human nature can be dialogic. As well, communication takes a leading role in our lives. This would be creation and liberation. Non-dialogic actions can refuse dialogue, misshape communication and demonstrate power.

THE DIALOGICAL COMMUNICATION IS THE NATURE OF THE HUMAN BEING. IT IS NECESSARY TO DISTINGUISH BETWEEN THE TRULY DIALOGICAL –THOSE THAT DRIVE THE MUTE UNDERSTANDING– AND THOSE THAT ARE NOT BECAUSE THEY DENY DIALOGUE AND DEMONSTRATE POWER OF SOME OVER OTHERS.

HABERMAS

In recent years there have been many advances in the use of dialogic learning. Learning communities have grown like freely fertilised wild mushrooms -in different context. Organizations seek transformation in their procedures and municipalities. They encourage citizens' participation. Both examples demonstrate free participation,

We propose the dialogical approach to be as a dialogue between equals without constraints, negations or debates. We understand it as the sum and inclusion of all visions and proposals.

In this approach we must ensure that all participants feel free and interested in participating. All participants must know their opinions in advance so their contributions will not fall on to deaf ears. Each one of them will be taken into consideration on equal footing.

The role is participatory and acceptor of diversity, that is, all we add, we do not go against anyone, so we try to stop using the word 'no.'

We can say ideas that in principle seem contrary but positive. The mountain can be high or low because each person will explain his or her vision of the issue from his or her vital perspective.

But neither are we going to go crazy and ask everyone everything. Pay attention. Let's not get excited. Everything is measured appropriately and at the right moment.

We remember from one of our earliest childhood memories that first sayings we learned "Everything in its place, and a place for everything".

We shamelessly confess and regret that we still do not know if we have passed that first kindergarten lesson as perhaps the reader can appreciate our messy and baroque style of writing.

If we apply the wise and practical saying to our approaches, the first thing that should be established is that each of the approaches has its corresponding applications -because we are always open to proposals that increase or improve them.

Let's not do this like the drunken man in the joke who was looking for his keys under the streetlamp of the street. A policeman tried to help him, he asked where he thinks he had lost them. The drunken man said, 'most likely in the park.' The policeman asked 'why?' This is when the drunken man replied, 'this is where the light is.' This is an analogy that demonstrates one must not use the same approach for all problems. Do not always use the hammer thinking that all problems are nails.

While it is true that there are polyvalent approaches almost as versatile as duct tape - we must acknowledge one thing about this item; that since the discovery of its diversity and possible uses, we are its most ardent supporters and do not lose the opportunity to use it nor to comment on it.

For this reason, we propose to use the dialogical approach when we want to listen to the voice of all, to collect everyone's general and particular vision.

It is an approach to be used whenever plurality is an added value. For example, when diagnosing the existing network or when collecting the proposals for the design of the proposed network or, for a cool brainstorming.

If used, the best procedure must be foreseen in each case, although very often the dynamics of small groups are used, and they gradually converge into the general group. There is an inhibition of those who hold power so that no voice is mediated or distorted.

Something like a cascade effect with antigravity, that is, just the reverse of the cascade effect of pyramidal procedures which is logical because it's on the opposite end of the spectrum.

PAPERBAGE

The Diverse Approach

Homeostatic balance – an important characteristic of open systems that will be later discussed in the Systemic approach – it is used in biology to refer to the level of fluid and biochemical elements that the human body should retain within certain ranges without raising any alarms.

That is what happens to us during, and after a crazy night. After night, the euphoria that alcohol gives us comes with a morning hangover and some sincere regrets. After the rush comes, then comes the downer. After an indigestion of diversity, plurality comes the day after. Why in some moments, if we cannot even stand ourselves, how can we put up with crap from others?

At this point, it is when Sartre's famous dictum *the hell is others* comes to mind. A phrase that interests us as it is the difficulty of understanding the viewpoint of others.

If we start from the basis of a plural network, the immediate consequence is the plurality of the visions of reality. The plurality of shared visions and knowledge emerges from that point.

Expressed like this, it sounds nice, but many will tell us: What does one do to understand one's neighbour? How can I help them better understand what I say?

If everyone gives opinion the natural tendency is to want to defend your own castle. This is until people get sick of us and can only agree to disagree. It depends on the character of each person, of course.

There will be people who will always agree with you and people who will never do.

If competitiveness arises, rather than cooperation we are closer to guerrilla warfare than to a collaborative network.

And Watzlawick warned us when, in the pathologies of communication, he pointed at scalation among equals. This can happen when a symmetrical relationship - of similar functions- people fall in tough competition. When it comes to who gets the upper hand, there is no possible collaboration.

Also, with personal disagreements, remember that the level of relationship between people, according to Watzlawick, prevails and is above the level of content communication- leading to disagreements on content.

Or, conversely, good relations make us change our opinions, in detriment of plurality. All of this is known to us. Well that is- if you are my friend... do not contradict me, boy oh boy!

We're talking about communicating different views that can be adopted by others. Otherwise... What is the network for, right?

We propose a different approach, changing the role of people unchaining themselves from their initial visions or proposals to make them participants in other different ones, even making them responsible for their development to better understand these opinions and to be able to advance with them.

As an exercise. Temporarily. It is not a brain transplant or empathising or anything like that. It is about changing optics, where I stand and what I see from here.

This approach can be applied to a small meeting with very specific goals or (take another case), exchanging tasks or functions among several people in an organization.

It is an unusual way to understand the processes that happen around us, processes we want and we think we know, but we do not know about in great depth.

The Reverse Approach

Machado said that in Spain, nine out of ten people butt heads and only one thinks. The fact that he had to live during terrible times such as the Civil War makes his pessimism totally understandable.

There are days in which we completely agree with him and others we think it is no big deal.

No need to be Solomonic, we do observe certain natural tendencies to seek the contrary, external enemies, those *others* who do not know or are not like us.

In any community we can find two opposing sides- apparent opposing sides. One side preaches against the other, postulates its disappearance or its diminution to the minimum expression.

Because sometimes, they are not interested in the complete disappearance of the opposite, what matters is to win. The disappearance of the opponent could be the beginning of the end itself. If there were no illnesses, we would not need doctors.

We witness such patterns in several areas. In politics, we have the left and the right. In football, teams are unmatched when it comes to rivalry. And, there are many other aspects of life in which you can see this- science can oppose religion. We could go on and on with many other examples of antagonism.

We would need to analyse in some of these cases if there is more to being an antagonist. We would have to consider them as complements.

We know that extremes meet, right? Or is that really the case? We discovered this in elementary

Geography class. Oh, and people say going to school is worthless - when we were taught that Asia and the Americas met in the Bering Strait, when you were told that the two points furthest from the map hanging above the blackboard were actually together. *Because, remember, the world is a sphere and this map should actually be rolled up* - added the Professor. Since that day, we looked differently at that map, we turned our heads nearly 360 degrees to try to join the two ends.

We propose to apply the inverse approach in these dichotomist situations where we are in a dilemma between yes or no, black or white.

This is a particular application of the diverse approach. Do remember that the diverse approach applies to different visions, but they do not have to be contrary. However, the reverse refers to only two positions seen as antagonistic.

We are aware of the gross simplification that often can result in the choice between black and white. Where is the grey option? And the other colours?

The first thing to pose as a preamble to this approach is just that- the diverse approach. If the dilemma persists, then apply the reverse.

We propose to exchange the roles as the diverse. A priori, may be more complex than in the diverse one as the positions are more encoded, but if the role play is carried out honestly and with parity, the results can be faster.

At this point someone -usually, the background-can counter the argument saying: *these roles are ok but let us see how they are regulated because we are all as we are, and everyone does as they like, or at least, I will do as I like.*

The regulation of approaches is reserved for the end - we will reply - it will be the icing of approaches-Yourself.

The Systemic Approach

Sometimes our memory plays tricks on us. We forget the most important and the most unimportant things we remember. It is like a little girl having fun playing with our memories as if they were toys, changing places, groping, transforming them, cornering them...

Like one of those random moments starring our naughty friend that we've kept at the *far, far, far, far* back of our memory like a far-off galaxy from *Star Wars*. That time in which a friendly and clueless bearded professor explained to us closed and open systems. It was good for us at the time that this fell into our hands, but it was too many years ago, and there's less memory regarding the General Systems Theory.

Because seeing it from our perspective today surely, we can continue reading as to recognize some of those concepts, something has clicked in our neurons.

What you were told when you were small *You still don't know but you will understand when you are older* which of course bothered you immensely back then and now you see that you're saying the same thing. Something like that happened to us.

It was not the first time we associated a link to the past, something that had had some internal logic - that is why we remembered it- but totally disconnected from anything we knew in our childhood. Suddenly that voice in your head started telling you that the pieces fit, it was engraved -isolated among other memories- it took relevance.

The logic of systems has trapped us. We immediately saw the connection of open systems with communicative situations. In other words, this theory or part of it could help us in understanding the elements of communication.

Step by step, as we have extended our readings, we discover the work done at the University of Palo Alto by many valuable scientists that have formulated the Theory of Human Communication.

There is nothing more practical than a good theory a phrase given by Kurt Lewin- so it has been in our case.

Now we start from the basis of considering communicative action as an open system and the practical consequences that we draw from it are various

If we apply the properties of open systems to communicative situations, we can find many possibilities.

For example, if we apply circularity in communicative action, it helps us to imagine it, to represent it or to draw it as a circular succession, as a more or less complex cycle in which we can apply various approaches., as a more or less complex cycle in which we can apply various approaches.

The systems approach is a descriptive basis, a practical visual and very effective way in which can work. This approach becomes the cornerstone in which we can base a whole series of communicative approaches, using, combining and manipulating the characteristics of the elements present in such cycles.

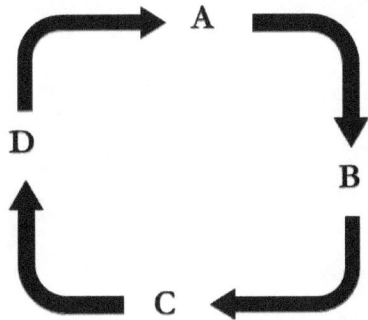

A cycle that can be used to express communicative actions, applying the principle of circularity.

If we apply the ownership of totality and equifinality, underlining the interconnectedness of all elements of the system, and that this same result can be achieved in different ways, (in such a way that any change in one of them can have repercussions on the others), we can apply the transformative approach. The so called 'Senge archetypes' are a good and inspiring example, as they show a representation of the practices and procedures we desire.

If we apply the circularity property, we have several options to mark off at the beginning of the process, as many elements as there are in the cycle. Because, strictly speaking, in a cycle there is no beginning or end. At least, not an obvious one.

All these properties and their consequences are discussed below.

The Different Score Approach

I didn't start it, he did, was one of our handiest sentences for self-defence when we were in trouble for something. It is interesting how little we already knew of the importance of the order of the factors - except in multiplication- altering the result.

At that time, it seemed grossly unfair to receive the same punishment as the initiator of the mischief, the one to blame. Adults had a timeless and disorderly sense of justice or so it seemed to us then.

Does the order of the sequence matter so much? Excuse me. Not the order, but where do you start? Apparently, it does. According to researchers at Palo Alto, most marital problems stemmed from this one thing. We're like children indeed!

Couples living in a state of mutual criticism and their feedback was the subject of numerous investigations. Apparently, there is no doubt that the lack of agreement on the sequence of events - that is, who or what was the first, whether it was chicken or the egg - resulted in problems of communication

If we consider the circularity and resourcefulness of the facts, it is difficult to distinguish between causes and consequences, and the consequences are in turn causes of the following event in the cycle. And of course, back again. It is like the fish biting its tail. What we usually call a 'vicious circle.'

The way to resolve this is via leaving the circle. There is no other solution to the problem.

However, what for some is a source of problems, for us, is a solution.

We propose that once the corresponding cycle is identified and represented in response to systemic approach, we proceed to identify what Senge calls the 'lever system.' The lever that satisfactorily manages to resolve the cycle.

We propose distributing the cycle with all possible scores. There will be as many start up options as there are in the cycle.

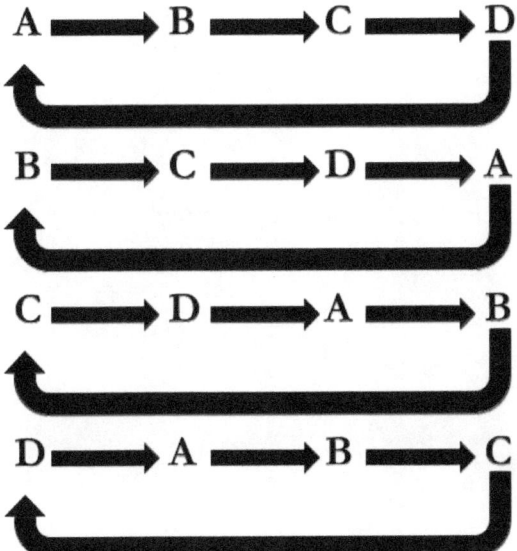

Communicative sequences with different starting points, applying the different score approach.

They should be distributed among the participants to reflect on their consequences beforehand.

All findings of all variants with other participants in the form and manner provided, which can be according to interest- a different approach that would enrich the previous analysis are then shared.

The Transformative Approach

As we love to use film references to encourage a readable introduction, this chapter will make use of two quick-change artists, namely Mystique and Transformers. Do you know them?

Mystique, a metamorphic X-men character, can change her form and acquire the appearance of anyone else. It's a super power that amazed us in comics but after seeing her in movies, it amazed us even more. Special effects have advanced to such a degree that Mystique's transformations are amazingly real.

Transformers have also become very successful regardless of exceeding their dynamism and the noises they made. It was a little too strident for our taste although we do understand its success among young people.

We would like to have a bit of their abilities to be transformative in our surrounding reality. Just a pinch. That is what we are here for.

If we have identified the components of the system using the systemic approach and represented the representative cycle of the sequence of events that interest us, we can take the next step.

We propose to transform these components according to the principles of totality and equifinality. That is, if the result can be the same, let's change the elements to analyse the changes that occur in the chain. We may be interested in achieving the same result but with more efficiency or economically intermediate steps. The interest may be another, i.e., even getting a different and better endpoint. Depending on the goal, we will act accordingly.

Let's make a prior distribution of all components among participants, asking about the prior development from each one of them. We can ask them to have a transformation. We can ask them to use paradigmatic elements interchangeable and syntagmatically related within the structure.

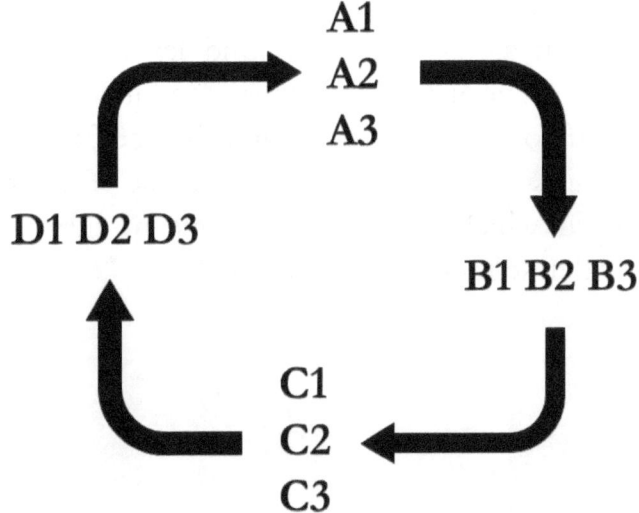

Relations are syntagmatic in the same class (A1, A2, A3...) and paradigmatic with the others. The transformative approach can change one for others, distributing, to its convenience, the roles that each one represents among the participants.

If they are interchangeable because they belong to the same class, they will have a paradigmatic relationship. If they can relate to those of a different class, they will have a syntagmatic relationship.

When we talk about classes, we are referring to almost any classification that may occur whenever we maintain the internal coherence of the analysis process. As an example, class `A' could be people, 'B' could be circumstances, `C 'could be actions and` D' might be modes of action.

It is certainly the most complex of all our proposed approaches. It requires prior mastery of various concepts of systems theory developed by Senge. Mainly of reinforcement and negative compensation along with delay and lever. Here is another good opportunity to review the bibliography at the end if you want to delve into this specific issue.

We think it is particularly suitable for key moments in which organizations have to turn the course or define their strategic lines.

The Divergent Approach

Innovating is trendy. We all aim to innovate. Everyone wants to innovate, they know how to innovate, they are the Kings and Queens of innovation, but when it comes to proving it, it seldom becomes reality.

The truth is that very few people know, can, and innovate. Most people copy reset and talk a lot.

They sell smoke. Empty Words. *Nihil novum sub solem* the classics would say. For those who neither know nor want to learn Latin: *Nothing new, old man,* or something like that...

It was said a few decades that the Japanese didn't innovate, all they did was miniaturise, i.e. copy products, and reduce them in size.

We believe that it is not as common as before, we do not know if that is because they do not do it anymore or because everyone does it.

Nor was it so bad if it was true cause they managed to miniaturise things without losing other qualities. But we are now going big, it doesn't matter if it works. A great example would be smartphones.

We think the road is out of the way, i.e., when you travel where everyone else goes, there is no possibility of innovation.

That saying goes *it's stupid to think that a different result will be achieved doing the same thing* is often attributed to Einstein.

That is obvious-the difference is in the different. We have not discovered America. We also copy, in a good way, we use other people's ideas trying to change them, modify them and give them a new meaning. We believe that innovation is in the details, in small major changes in elements that are minimal in appearance.

We also believe that we must take into consideration-that is, to take some time to think- what the weird guy in the corner says, the guy that's alone. The guy who doesn't seem too cool. That guy nobody understands when he is speaking and when he is understood -very occasionally- his opinion goes against the common opinion or is perceived as 'nonsense,' it just so happens it is the farthest from innovation.

When someone goes against the general opinion and says something incomprehensible, he or she is either very smart or very stupid. Well, this is what most people think. It's the natural reaction, according to the previous reputation of the subject, there may be admiring judgment or a negative bias.

But this doesn't need to be so, it may be because of different experiences, unknown premises ... For instance, someone much older can surprise a young person -often negative, of course, and vice versa-that is, that the young person can also surprise the older person, in most cases, negatively. There may also be similar situations that occur between people from very different backgrounds and cultures.

We also believe that innovation is not based on improvisation, but one cannot deny it can play the flute without music lessons, but we find it unlikely a melody will emerge from it.

We believe that to innovate requires a context, an ecosystem, fertile soil that is well maintained, planted, ploughed and irrigated. And as knowledge emerges from the network, innovative knowledge arises from the designed network, the dedicated spaces, the shared personal and collective networks, the habits, approaches and ways that are employed.

We propose to apply the procedures outlined in the previous pages. We propose to apply the dialogic approach to expand the range and collect the plural options in our network.

We propose to apply the transformative approach, noting clearly the big picture, to identify and analyse key processes.

We propose to apply the different approach to understand emerging knowledge sharing. And, if innovation has not emerged throughout this journey, we can apply the divergent approach.

We can consider the divergent approach as a particular hybrid development between the transformative approach and the diverse approach. It is about considering the steps and elements identified in the transformative approach and, after making the necessary -weird, different and surprising- changes, we can allocate roles according to the different approach previously explained.

The divergent approach is a set of different situations -networks and spaces- and a succession of approaches. Anywhere or anytime can be surprising.

The intelligent observer recognises and distinguishes the emerging knowledge that participants share in existing networks so diligently.

PAPERBAGE

The Attributive Approach

Fair play is a concept used based on competitive sports, so it is not surprising that we also use it for other human activities in which there are interactions, struggles and attempts at improvement.

Within any organization, we have little disagreements, minor confrontations ..., and at times real fratricidal wars between gangs and cliques.

For personal motives, I love you Andres. This is a Spanish saying in which Andres is the multi-millionaire, and his romantic partner is interested in his millions, not love. This is one of the most commonly used sayings when we want to talk about a a relationship of convenience, or a lack of true love. People are often driven by selfish motives, regardless of others and the advancement of their group.

Was Rousseau right to say that a man - or woman in her case- is innocent in nature at time of birth and then she becomes evil over time?

So, who corrupts man? According to Rousseau, wealth and power were the main causes.

But if Rousseau was right or not, the state of affairs has not changed much if anything at all. We could add some collaborating factors in this moral degeneration.

Hercule Poirot, the misogynist, said *cherchez la femme,* referring to the motive for murders that he investigated and happily solved. Love, rather than deception and heartbreak, envy, laziness or natural tendency of many to *dolce far niente.* Money, power, many are the temptations and known motives for selfishness, self-deceit and even crime.

Nash, the one with a beautiful mind from that movie we saw a few years ago, the special guy who scientifically demonstrated his famous *Nash equilibrium,* the milestone known as 'Game Theory,' in which he theorised that the selfishness of people could only be overcome by some sort of standard, pre-established communication or reasoning. And he showed that when he demonstrated to his colleagues a winning strategy when it came to the difficult art of flirting. He proposed a strategy that was based on the agreement of suitors. The agreement was that none of them would try to flirt with the prettiest one. That way, they would not offend the other and everyone would be able to pick up a girl.

Actually, we do not know how it ended nor have we applied the recipe until today -we went for it- the first and only time, to the most beautiful and, we must add, that we did so successfully.

Another good example of this principle is the famous prisoner's dilemma. Two prisoners are held incommunicado, so that the police offer a good deal to who collaborates first. The first one to rat out on the other goes free or gets a reduced sentence in return for his collaboration with law officers, while the other one who is the most faithful to his buddy, the lesser of the traitors, would get far worse and receive a long sentence.

If both remain silent and maintain mutually loyal to one another, both will escape with just a small punishment. The result almost always, as the police know well -among other existing reasons, which is why they were held incommunicado - is that the detainees will rat on one another sooner or later.

With one exception. What is the exception, that in which detainees don't rat each other out? It is straightforward. When the benefits of ratting each other out are lower than the potential harm.

For example, both detainees are members of a larger gang or mafia, those who are tempted to rat know that revenge will be taken upon them wherever they go, even under the protection of the famous witness protection programme, as we can see in many crime movies.

Game theory and *Nash equilibrium* cannot prove natural child innocence or Rousseau-like claims, but it makes clear to us that the structure of standards and rules -written in ink, blood or word -known to all members of an organization can foster more ethical and cooperative behaviour.

In other words. You must help the group. Perhaps Rousseau got it right ... we're not kids anymore.

We propose that ethical dimension be the basis of all human activity. It works for us- religious, secular, and other ethics.

We affirm that as far as this issue is concerned, ethics based on altruism is ephemeral, and that the enduring ethic is one based on justice, on equal opportunities, on the correct application of rules, and on fair giving of credit.

Giving credit is the key to the vault, the crux of the matter, within an organization that wants to share knowledge.

We consulted a webpage on the internet that provides rhymes for any word (rimador.net); if you are not familiar with it go and look it up, it's 'da bomb.' We have five key words here because the act of 'attribution' (giving credit), rhymes with: contribution, distribution, redistribution and retribution.

These attributions- let's give credit to those who have shared knowledge via the ability to do so or with his or her own ingenuity.

If a superior or boss takes credit for something he or she has done unjustly; many times, there are short, medium and long-term consequences which are difficult to quantify.For instance, a disgruntled employee who underperforms nor has any inkling to perform; or perhaps, a vengeful worker who hinders the work of the group by hiding their progress. There are also many dumb, passive and lazy workers who do not want to contribute so others can claim glory, receive promotions. and gain prizes.

All of this is seasoned with irreconcilable hatreds, apparent inabilities to mutually help one another, and no sharing of knowledge.

What is giving credit? Of course, we are speaking about giving credit to someone. I mean, perhaps a pat on the shoulder? Or, are we talking about more tangible and material issues? The arbitrariness of giving credit to a bad employer's agreement, the wanting to do so, and then 'I cannot.' The praises and other soapy paraphernalia which have a very short run till you turn the next corner. And for this reason, we were better than before.

This is one of the main characteristics of any organization that wants knowledge to be shared. This is surely the most levelling characteristic, it's more equalising, so why not disclose it? We can make it a tad more unpleasant for the bosses.

Well, the answer is because it questions their status, this is how they feel. It bothers them that subordinates take credit since it seems that it somehow discredits them and makes them look bad.

But it is the other way around, it's the boss or superior who accredits marksmanship, who masterfully delivers, and who generously contributes more than anyone else.

When all is said and done, clarity and precision are essential. All members should know what they earn when they contribute and know how contributions are measured and valued. And everyone should be able to know how sharing is valued, even though it doesn't yield immediate and visible results. We propose that the attributive approach be explained and applied, since it will be the necessary fuel for knowledge to flow in the network.

PAPERBAGE

The Training Approach

What is the company culture of most organizations like regarding the training of its members?

In many of them it is about vicarious learning, to learn by imitation, or it's experiential which is learning by practice. This is always focused on the newcomers so that they can be integrated as soon as possible into company culture.

Later they jump from one thing to another, just like bees that hop from one flower to the flower, birds that peck at a tree and then fly to the other, generally being fostered by happy ideas from overrated bosses.

Who designs the training? Who proposes it? Who has it? Who has the idea? Are they, perhaps the most seasoned because it is already known that 'with age comes wisdom?' Or is it better for us to be young because the boldness of youth is a powerful and valid tool in this day and age?

We propose that the personal network is one way of training and that their sharing helps to determine the general guidelines.

For the same reason we propose that there be a programmed training approach and an unprogrammed one.

Remember that the network allows for unforeseen situations and that at any moment something unexpected could occur. Remember that it is impossible not to communicate, learn and train. Serendipity, informal and unforeseen learning can arise at any time and happen unexpectedly, by associations of ideas at any time and place. This can plant the seed for the beginning of the best proposals.

We propose that newcomers immerse themselves in the philosophy of the organization, in the ways of its functioning and in the existing networks. This will be their best training, and this is also where they will contribute their new visions to everyone.

It's also appropriate to apply the dialogical approach when programming broad or generalised training processes, even if it is only to detect the training needs from different points of view.

Following this, it will be necessary to use the deliberative approach to deliberate the best options.

Another practical option that drives learning and experiential training is the use of the diverse approach, exchanging functions for predetermined periods of time between different people in order to be trained through directed practices.

It is training together with information - not the concealment of it, nor fear and disinformation - that achieves transformation in an organization. A training that is continuous, well-structured and better led which meets the real needs of people and groups.

IT IS TRAINING TOGETHER WITH INFORMATION –NOT THE CONCEALMENT OF IT, NOT FEAR AND DISINFORMATION– THAT ACHIEVES TRANSFORMATION IN AN ORGANIZATION.

PAPERBAGE

The Deliberative Approach

We are going to do a simplification exercise. Let's do this just like how there are those people who divide the world into two categories. Let's say in the way that there are those who prefer orange soda or those who prefer lemon. Those who use deodorant and those who do not. Those who sing in the shower or those who do not. Okay?

Okay we are good to go; our dilemma is between the determined minded and the indecisive.

The determined ones have everything sectioned off. They're the ones who have everything clear. They know what their favourite colour is, what brand of car they like and how much they will have. They say many things like this: *In all my life ... There is nothing better* (whatever) *than ...* and they give advice - almost like orders in how to live life. Trust me, you know them when you see them... As you understand, these are the guys who like to make decisions. It doesn't matter whether they buy bread, go on vacation or it's a work-related matter.

Now, let's have a look at the indecisive group. They live in a sea of doubts. Everything seems doubtful. They give the impression of being quite insecure in deciding on what steps to take. *This one? No! It's the same but the next one is better! Oh! But what if it's not like that? I don't know if ...*, these are their go-to expressions.

Normally these expressions are accompanied by deciding what to do after what they are told to do. Of course, after taking some time to do so.

Make up your mind! We don't have all day. Oh, what patience is needed to handle you! Not even Mother Theresa could have endured as much as we did!

If you have had the fortune of being with someone from this group -which is not difficult to come by since they must number in the millions. We believe that they number almost the same amount as those of the determined group- you have surely heard curses, whinging and similar complaints, go figure- almost on any subject.

The biggest problem arises when (as you imagine), when we put together a couple from the same group. Imagine two from the indecisive group. Oh, what a pain in the butt and what a waste of time! Now imagine two indecisive ones put together. Oh, what arguments and how bothersome!

We think that the indecisive one always get away with it and, depending on how you look at, they are the most determined because they always decide on the same thing, that is they let the others decide and then if something doesn't work, they will put the blame on them.

We think that the decision-making process, the deliberations to select the best option correspond in principle to the heads of the organization, to the shareholders, to the partners, to the general assembly or to those who delegate.

Decision making is a manifestation of power. It is the upmost manifestation of power. It is power in all its splendour, although it is taking into account and in highly considering the proposals of the subordinates.

That is why it agrees with whoever corresponds according to the subject matter and as specified by the statutes, laws or corresponding norms.

By all means, we are not going to skip the hierarchy. We are clear that a decision does not have to be democratic.

Or yes. It depends on many factors, some of which we have detailed because we are very clear that it has to be explained.

We propose that we must describe who will make the decision, when it will be done, how, and why. Actually, we propose that if it's possible, it should be described as thoroughly as possible.

We propose to always (or almost always), separate the deliberative process from any other approach, meeting or activity. Remember that power distorts everything. It's like the sun or a massive star that doubles space-time. It's like a black hole that swallows all ideas before they appear.

That is why we propose to explain a priori the details of the deliberative approach which is clearly separated from all main tasks or activities, meetings, work, proposals, etc. Be that approach or another, once the meetings are over, convene the deliberations as a separate development, separately - perhaps immediately following all of the above. And in the end, communicate the results.

Let's not act like that boss who wanted to give his workers democratic and pluralist explanations of the matter at hand. This boss said that he considered everyone's opinion but before giving the floor to anyone he made it clear to them his position on the matter! He even predicted disasters in case they didn't follow his directions, and he was expecting plurality, what a joke!

Unfortunately, and surely, this may ring a bell since everybody (one way or another), has slid in their criteria before asking for your opinion.

Another typical pathology occurs when apart from not separating the decision-making process, no clear decision is made. It's left floating in the air so that almost every participant interprets it in his or her own way. Because as there is no protocol... in the end, what does it serve? Isn't that true?

Avoid similar situations and give explanations at the right times.

The *a priori* explanation avoids uncertainty. If at the beginning of a meeting we do not know who will decide, personnel will be displaced, and this is far from phenomenal. Each one acts according to his or her own hypothesis, some according to the a previously mentioned custom, others according to his or her own personal criteria. However, misunderstandings and fears will be present.

The *a posteriori* explanation avoids the arbitrary sensation that occurs if the reasons that have been taken into account in the resolution method are not given.

THE EXPLANATION
A PRIORI
AVOIDS
UNCERTAINTY,
THE EXPLANATION
AFTERWARD
AVOIDS
THE SENSATION OF
ARBITRARINESS.

PAPERBAGE

In addition, it is advisable whenever the topic lends itself to it, to consult the people involved so those who understand the subject can provide clues that help us make decisions.

For this reason, it will be necessary to first consider the functions they perform and follow the logical steps without any bypassing. We must take into consideration the personnel directly affected.

We must remember that we all like to be kept in mind and this also results in greater identification and personal involvement. If we actively listen to someone, it may be easier for them to feel that their decision is theirs.

If we previously commented about the dialogical approach being overrated, it is at this point that we would like to be rehabilitated and wear our new Sunday dress to our current welcome consensus. Of course, there is nothing better than a good consensus-based decision made by us all!

If we have the necessary time and the necessary desire; and above all, the subject is important enough - we can apply the diverse approach that oils up deliberations, opens the minds, and predisposes even the most stubborn.

Be that as it may, an individual decision carries more risks of being valued less than a collective one, but a collective one may take more time and not be as efficient as it is intended.

We have already commented on the importance of *a posteriori* communication, to which we should add the responsibility of the people who will have to implement the decision in question, if it is one, several or all. And their level of involvement according to the participation in the previous process.

It depends on how you look at it, everything that is spoken is not more than that, until it is carried out only in words.

In addition, someone has to control the effectiveness of the decisions and propose planned actions according to the level of execution with the possibility of adjustments and subsequent changes.

The forecast has to look at everything until the end, including consequences of the decisions in the general climate, taking responsibility in case bad decisions are made-if it is a single and clearly identifiable person, a small group or a large group in which future proposals are diluted...etc.; for which will come (and be more than welcome), an adaptive approach that will retrofeed the entire process.

The Adaptive Approach

Adapt or die which is the purest and hardest reality of Darwinism. Or, no matter how much adaptive ability you have, *'life is too short for souvenirs,'* which goes after all you souvenir collectors.

With that we want to suggest that the opposite is feasible, adapt and die, but we will discuss that later.

We know how this film ends and there is no *nothing lasts forever-* no eternal company, nor an immortal being. This is a fact.

Lately, this is something we've been hearing about. Technological singularity which is or will be the moment in which computers surpass the computational capacity of the human brain. This could lead us to a splendid future with our immortal lives joined to machines as an 'all-in-one' being. If not, this will be our disappearance or extinction caused by intelligent machines as was predicted in the dystopia that was bestowed upon us so many years ago, the Terminator trilogy. However, life goes on.

Anyways, we are just messing with the reader. The adaptive approach is all about feedback. This is the approach that monitors and adapts the system. It is a subsystem or a part of the systemic approach and for the same reason it is intimately linked with the transformer.

Of course, it is also related to the homeostatic equilibrium mentioned in these approaches, since a part of the system is redirected to the entrance of the system to control its behaviour.

It is the positive feedback that is reinforced and leads to saturation. The negative feedback readjusts and leads to stabilisation.

It is a system of controlling systems. Control points are designed and implemented for system feedback.

They are sets of circular sequences whose components are moments, places, indicators or controllers.

Let's not confuse this language of positive and negative and assimilate it into praise and reproach. It has nothing to do with it. They have very different meanings.

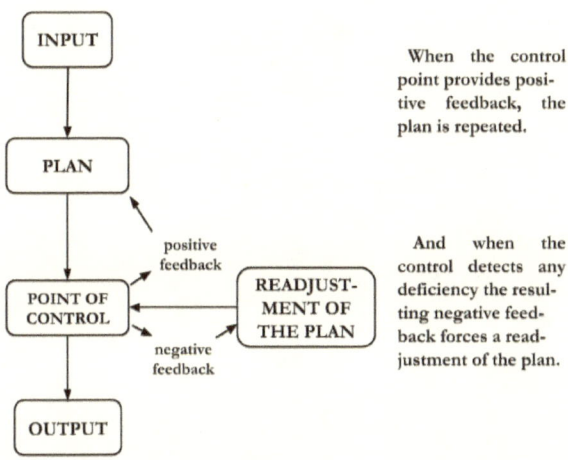

When the control point provides positive feedback, the plan is repeated.

And when the control detects any deficiency the resulting negative feedback forces a readjustment of the plan.

Positive feedback reinforces non-change and negative transformation-nothing more and nothing less.

It sounds dictatorial, straitjacketed, very black and white and inelastic which is very far from our intention. We are not talking about an automatic control carried out by machines. We are talking about control directed by people who continually question all aspects and explore all possibilities.

We propose that the plan is 'no-plan," and what should be rewarded is the work of criticism and control that leads to continuous change.

Of course, there is a plan, but it changes without fear. Controls should provide information about system failures and offer solutions or pave the way for them to occur. They must be designed in such a way that it's not worth clinging to the known.

It is necessary to establish mechanisms of the diverse approach in the controls. It should be done in such a way that people change their functions and roles of control and are compensated for their discoveries of defective points. This can be very frowned upon.

Like a canary in a coalmine, killing the messenger who delivers bad news was the typical things to do in medieval times. Indeed, we are confronted with a very human characteristic, that in which one doesn't want to cater to dissonant points of view, that of not wanting to see what we should change, because it is more optimistic, less negative—and more comfortable- having a more optimistic view.

Sometimes it is the words we use that lead us to deception. Who is the scoundrel who wants to see everything in black and live in a world of pessimism? We certainly do not want this, and we suppose you don't either. Change the approach and change the words used. It is a very basic error of approach.

How should we be optimistic and have a positive vision? Not in the 'unwanting' to see or not being objective, but the other way around. It is about finding improvements and proposing changes.

This kind of information is key. For this reason, we must design a system of adaptive controls that reward people who put their finger on the pulse. There are several well-known sayings that express this idea: *to hope for the best and anticipate the worst, the best is the enemy of the good*, etc. No, but let us remember the power of words and we can rectify these sayings. We choose the adaptive approach that aims to transform the existing plan which is already good, and we will try and do better. Everything will be positive, and nothing will be negative.

Many organizations have wanted to improve their relationship with customers, internal processes, training for workers, and their productivity. They've been dragged, pushed, and sometimes trapped and overwhelmed by the so-called 'quality processes' in such a way that in recent decades they have created a monopoly as most organizations' attention is focused on having a praiseworthy objective based on improvement, evaluation and the readjustment of plans thus improving the processes they perform.

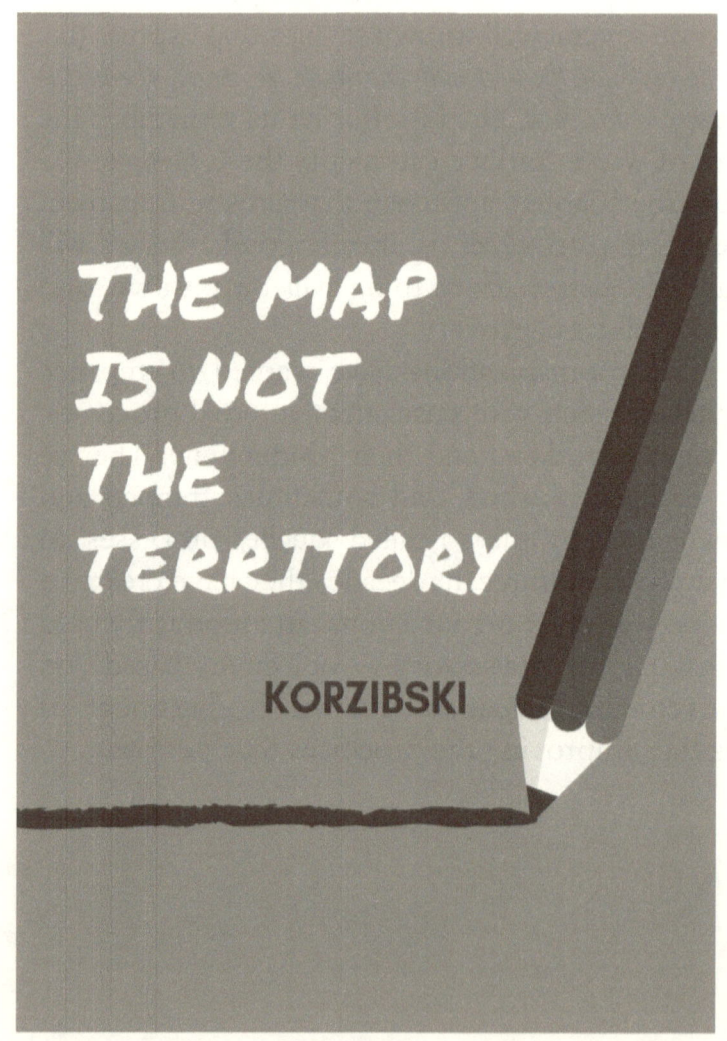

Some love to brag about ISOS and EFQM and other such frameworks that provide quality control. They're seen as *cool*, and they're worshipped. Especially in marketing where it's highly adored.

Let's clarify this, there's been a wave, a tsunami that began where the mother of all tsunamis began, in Japan.

It was them who created this standard. The objective they had which according to our understanding was to produce the exact quantity, or at least as close as possible to the total amount of sales; that is, to adjust the production and quantity in time and *just in time*.

This seems to be it and not another source of all this paranoia regarding quality processes. Although naturally this thing evolved, diversified and became more complicated.

Who knows why we go along with the children of the Rising Sun? We could have done the same as the Japanese strikes, that is, to take the idea and flip it around like a sock - although as far as we know the latter is nothing more than a happy urban legend.

No, what we have done was the start of a course of procedures, evaluations and quality indicators, that although in some cases led us to reflect and improve the work we did; in other cases, it led us to a significant increase in paperwork and bureaucracy. We remember the importance they gave to documenting all the processes, right down to the tiniest detail. What is not written does not exist, they said. 'Come write and document everything, record it all, duplicate it, or perhaps better if you triplicate it, do it schematically and in prose, both in digital format and on paper.'

We come from this kind of culture. We are a people who discovered that a job well done had to be documented.

In the past, the power of the written word was a kind of truth revealed that was inaccessible to the illiterate. It was the Lord and Master of our perception of reality.

We immerse ourselves in that vortex of paper and cellulose, of records and graphics just like the authentically possessed who have the faith of a convert.

Until one day we discovered that we had gone too far, but it wasn't that. As a certain someone said, 'paper holds everything.'

It seemed an element had created its own reality especially when some evaluators appeared, and they analysed the documentation without worrying about its supposed real parallels.

As an example, we will mention the case of a quality process evaluator who went to a company to check on its safety and hygiene standards. The evaluator who was hired by the company to do the evaluation, approved some documentation and ignored a broken door which he had perfectly seen because he had walked under it. Since the corresponding document certified conclusively that the door was in perfect condition, the case was closed, and it ensured the safety of the insulation of the entire facility.

The irony of the situation is the evaluator complied with his job, which was to check the documentation. The actual situation of the door was not within his remit thus not being his responsibility.

Now we propose that what is written does not exist.

This comes to mind and is in contradiction of all the above when we recall that aforementioned saying of Korzybski, *the map is not the territory*, a phrase that came to him during the First World War in which he had fallen in a hole with his fellow soldiers. This hole was not shown on his military maps.

To which Bateson added, *the name is not the thing named*, a phrase that brings us closer to the question at hand.

To what we would add, what is written does not exist. That it is an elegant way of saying that what is written does not correspond to the reality of the facts, or that it is simply a more or less fortunate interpretation, more or less exact, according to the observation skills of the writer.

We could go even further and ask ourselves if there is a reality that we are not observing, but we will leave this to the quantum physics experts.

The Austerity Approach

Efficiency, as we understand it, is what matters to us now, it is over-exertion, it is the superfluous use of scarce resources, it's using a sledgehammer to kill a nut.

However, efficiency happens when everything works without moving a finger, without practically consuming any energy.

Efficiency is a balance that balances from the abuse of inadequacy.

If it leans towards abuse, we can be effective, but it will be at the cost of detracting or diverting essential elements for other functions. This is best expressed in the wise saying *One cannot rob Peter to pay Paul.*

And if it falls on the side of inadequacy, that is, if by saving or obsessively cutting we don't reach this ... then we will have wasted all our efforts. At the end of the day this will create frustration, in addition to other negative consequences such as the loss of trust which is usually called the *austerity trap*. Because there are those who confuse austerity with stinginess, with primitivism and with each *man for himself* complex.

Obviously, without underestimating politicians they're already dealing with them. We also denounce the obtuse use of the concept of austerity employed in the last years of crisis. The austerity for *you and yours* and the abundance of *me and mine-* money used to rescue banks and lower wages for workers.

Any organization must consider what is worth spending on, what is worth investing in, in what they could scrimp out on ... even in times of crisis.

The identification of key processes depends on other approaches explained above, mainly systemic, transformer and divergent.

We think that a company is part of the social fabric in which it is located, in which it is part of its environment. It is not something outside even if it is an industrial plant located on the outskirts of the city. It is not foreign though its origin is distant; however, it is part of the landscape and must be committed to the culture, customs, idiosyncrasy and sustainability of the whole.

We propose that an organization should consider what it contributes to its social ecological system. It must consider that it should contribute and not provide. It must analyse what damages it inflicts on its operations. You must recognise how to avoid them.

Ecology is an important concept of our proposal. A momentarily viable organism, punctually successful, in an environment that is punishing, lacking a future, and has an expiration date.

We would like to present our particular vision on the subject. We think that this misunderstood ecology is promoted. It is an ecology in which recycling occupies the central place, a decision that from our point of view is wrong, since recycling should occupy the last place, that of the lesser evil, something to be avoided.

Recycling is like Pontius Pilate washing his hands. If you don't understand the religious analogy-you're guilty and you are trying to fix what you have previously done wrong.

Re-use. That's the secret. Without recycling, reusing is the central theme. Cleaner is not he who cleans more, but he who dirties less. Let's keep telling this to ourselves. It is efficiency with awareness that detects deficiency and solves it with sufficiency.

For all these reasons, we propose to apply the dialogical approach to identify the plurality of the points, moments and situations in which the criteria of exposed efficiency can be applied, both of those referring to the social environment and those related to eco-efficiency.

We propose to identify via the systemic approach which are the processes and key points to which we dedicate more available resources. In addition, we propose to do it periodically.

The Metacommunicative Approach

The prefix meta in Greek means *after* or *beyond*. Thus, metaphysics is understood as something beyond physics. It is used to give meaning of abstraction of the term that precedes it. Metalanguage is the language that deals with the language itself. In the same way, metacommunication is to perform abstractions (to be as concrete as possible in our case), about communication.

This new role is different from the previous ones. Until now, as far as we can explain, the participants in the roles must deal with the matter in question in whatever form it comes by- from the assigned role, but in this new role, novelty is ensured so that the rules of the game are met.

Like any game, the role-playing games we are proposing also require a referee or a stage director.

We have left this for the end, the key figure of our proposal. It shows all the approaches presented, and some more that we would like to continue developing; they will go on.

Consequently, we present you with the goal, the main figure of this work. Enter into play the person that will apply the metacommunicative approach again and again. The approach is par excellence, very cornerstone. The approach takes cares of the other approaches- the most *ultra* of approaches.

Who is it and how is the goal? Approach after approach, all of those we have proposed need guidance, someone who is mindful of the specific approach to be applied and its corresponding roles and criteria.

There are very observant people. These types of people are detail oriented. They don't ever look bored. They prefer not to participate directly-notaries, UN observers in international conflicts, sexual Voyeurs, etc.

There are others who besides observing, they participate a bit more. They not only observe, but they also take special care in the rules of the game. They are the referees in sports competitions. They are also the film and theatre directors in the world of entertainment.

They are supposed to be impartial and independent of the other participants, offering equanimity and wisdom in the application of standards.

It is your responsibility to ensure compliance with the rules and roles of each approach.

At the beginning, it is who explains the details of the communicative act, the proposed objective, the roles of the participants.

During the application of the respective approach, it is the one who interacts with the participants, moderates the discussions, structures the meeting, marks the times of the interventions ... But without interfering in the subject in question.

Allow us this cinematic digression to introduce the character- Frank Herbert, author of the *Dune* trilogy. He introduced to us the Bene Gesserit, a sisterhood of genetically evolved priestesses who regardless of their participation in the plot of this science fiction saga, they possessed a supernatural communication power. For them humans were transparent in their intentions, in their truths and in their lies. They also had a superpower called *the voice,* in which they used vowel modulations to make proposals that no one could refuse, almost as convincing as those of Marlon Brando in his role as 'The Godfather.'

Without going to these extremes, if nothing happens the goal will be the communication specialist.

Obviously, you must recognise the mechanisms of the metacommunication approach.

In the dialogical approach, it must be clear how to achieve all the aims and how to inhibit any distorting powers.

In the diverse approach, one must delegate them as custom made roles.

And it is this way for everything.

In addition, the battery of the communication pathology detector must be well charged, so it doesn't run out of power in the middle of the session. For this reason, you must know that at the touch of your fingertips are these given pathologies. Regarding this point, Watzlawick should be your main adviser.

This insightful researcher listed a series of situations that carried negative consequences for the smooth running of communication.

According to him, the challengers did communicate according to the axioms that determined success or failure, it depended on the type of relationship they had. He claimed that his investigations showed different levels of communication, on the one hand there was a relationship between them and, at a lower level, always subordinate to the previous one, another one, that being the content of the message. Thus, the message was always conditioned by the relationship of friendship or previous hatred.

It also demonstrated the existence of complementary functions, similar functions and contrary functions among the interveners.

All of these characteristics, both those of relationship and those of function, could lead to regrettable competitive escalations, to non-collaborative escalations, to disapproval and inconsideration, to disqualifications and to blockades.

We propose this goal to be a skilful warrior and driver that, who as a seasoned master of ceremonies, is always neutral in his relations and distant from the content, without going into the crux of the matter, it applies the rules to bring the communicative approach to fruition which is exactly what we hope you get with this book and this being said, this book comes to an end.

We hope we have achieved the goal we have set for ourselves at the beginning. We hope that we have conveyed everything that we had set out to do. Regards.

PAPERBAGE

Bibliography

Adell Segura, J. & Castañeda Quintero, L. (2010) *Los Entornos Personales de Aprendizaje (PLEs): una nueva manera de entender el aprendizaje.* Alcoy: Marfil – Roma TRE Universita degli studi. Available from https://digitum.um.es/jspui/bitstream/10201/1724 7/1/Adell%26Casta%C3%B1eda_2010.pdf

Aubert, A., Flecha, A., García, C., Flecha, R., y Racionero, S. (2008). *Aprendizaje dialógico en la sociedad de la información.* Barcelona: Hipatia Editorial.

Ausubel, D., Novak, J., y Hanesian, H. (2009). *Psicología educativa: un punto de vista cognoscitivo.* México, Trillas.

Camisón, C.; Cruz, S. y González, T. (2007): *Gestión de la calidad: conceptos, enfoques, modelos y sistemas.* Prentice Hall, Madrid.

De Ugarte, D. (2007) *El poder de las redes.* Madrid: El Cobre.

Dolan, S., Valle, R., Jackson, S. & Schuler, R. (2007). *La gestión de los recursos humanos. Cómo atraer, retener y desarrollar con éxito el capital humano en tiempos de transformación.* España: Mc Graw Hill.

Euler, L. (1736). *Solutio problematis ad geometriam situs pertinentis*. Available from http://eulerarchive.maa.org//docs/originals/E053.pdf

Flecha, R. (1997). *Compartiendo Palabras: el aprendizaje de las personas adultas a través del diálogo*. Barcelona: Paidós.

Freire, P. (1970). *Pedagogía del Oprimido*. Madrid: Siglo: XXI.

Habermas, Jürgen (1987). *Teoría de la acción comunicativa*. Madrid: Taurus.

Foucault, M. (octubre-noviembre de 1983) *Discourse and Truth: the Problematization of Parrhesia*. Recuperado de https://web.archive.org/web/20080509135742/http://www.foucault.info/$/parrhesia/

La toma de decisiones. Available from https://web.archive.org/web/20101216040910/http://www2.gobiernodecanarias.org/educacion/17/WebC/Apdorta/reunion.htm

Organizational charts. Available from https://commons.wikimedia.org/wiki/Category:Organizational_charts

Senge, P. M. (2005). *La Quinta Disciplina En La Práctica*. Barcelona: Granica.

Siemens, G. (2006). *Conociendo el conocimiento* (2010, traducción de Emilio Quintana, David Vidal, Lola Torres y Victoria A. Castrillejo [Grupo Nodos Ele]). Available from http://recursos.cepindalo.es/pluginfile.php/10515/ mod_resource/content/1/docs_curso/saberMas/Si emens.Conociendoelconocimiento.pdf

Vygotsky, L. S. (1995). *Pensamiento y Lenguaje*. Barcelona: Paidós.

Von Bertalanffy, Ludwig (1976). *Teoría general de los sistemas. Fundamentos, desarrollo, aplicaciones*. México: Fondo de Cultura Económica.

Watzlawick, P., Beavin Bavelas, J., Jackson, D. D. (1981). *Teoría de la comunicación humana. Interacciones, patologías y paradojas*. Barcelona: Herder.

Wiener, Norbert (1985). *Cibernética*. Barcelona: Tusquets.

The vignettes have been created using the online tool *Strip Generator*. The cover photo is from Josh Sorenson –free for personal and comercial use, no attribution required-(www.pexels.com).

PAPERBAGE

THE FISH IS IN THE NET

PAPERBAGE

www.ingramcontent.com/pod-product-compliance
Lightning Source LLC
Chambersburg PA
CBHW021817170526
45157CB00007B/2622